CLASSIC GUITAR VOLUME 1

1

MEL BAY

This Method has been created for the fulfillment of a great need. That need is a simp—   od classic guitar playing.

Although the author has been established as a modern guitar stylist, he has been associated with the classic guitar since the age of fourteen when he became a devoted student of the music and methods of Carcassi, Sor, Aguado, Carulli, Tarrega, Mertz and many other classic guitar masters.

The Mel Bay methods for the modern guitar have been received enthusiastically all over the world. Teachers using these methods have noted the volume of classic guitar music used in those methods.

The many requests for a classic guitar method carefully graded and easily understood has been the prime reason for the creation of this course of study.

Mel Bay

CD CONTENTS

1 Tune Up & Introduction (2:35)	17 The Builder/Page 23 (:31)
2 Sparkling Stella/Page 12 (:25)	18 Small Chord Etude/Page 23 (:26)
3 The Third Finger/Page 13 (:49)	19 Bass Solo/Page 24 (:34)
4 The Merry Men/Page 13 (:35)	20 Little Minuet/Page 24 (:59)
5 How Can I Leave Thee/Page 17 (:58)	21 Miuetto/Page 27 (1:05)
6 Andantino/Page 17 (:56)	22 Dawn/Page 27 (1:07)
7 The First String Waltz/Page 18 (1:06)	23 A Study in Eighths/Page28 (:57)
8 Six Pence/Page 18 (:45)	24 Waltz/Page 31 (1:37)
9 The Pick-up Note/Page 19 (1:53)	25 Playtime/Page 32 (1:04)
10 Etude/Page 19 (:48)	26 Balkan Nights/Page 32 (1:19)
11 A Study by Aguado/Page 20 (1:14)	27 Rain Drops/Page 33 (:44)
12 Follow the Leader/Page 21 (1:31)	28 Cradle Song/Page 33 (:48)
13 Alpine Echos/Page 21 (:39)	29 The Blue Tail Fly/Page 34 (:44)
14 Waltz/Page 21 (1:03)	30 Italian Air/Page 35 (1:23)
15 The Tie Waltz/Page 22 (:59)	31 Classic Dance/Page 35 (1:01)
16 The Chord Waltz/Page 23 (:57)	

32 Senorita/Page 37 (1:09)
33 Senora/Page 37 (1:58)
34 Andante/Page 38 (1:22)
35 The Gauchos/Page 39 (1:06)
36 A Serenade/Page 40 (1:00)
37 Austrian Hymn/Page 41 (1:28)
38 The Little Prince/Page 42 (1:04)
39 By the Moonlight/Page 42 (1:01)
40 The Foggy, Foggy Dew/Page 45 (:45)
41 A Waltz by Sor/Page 46 (:48)
42 Andante/Page 46 (1:32)
43 A Night in Madrid/Page 47 (:58)
44 Song by Aguado/Page 47 (1:18)
45 Waltz in E Minor/Page 48 (1:04)
46 Conchita/Page 48 (1:23)
47 A Closing Note from the Author (:12)

Visit us on the Web at http://www.melbay.com — E-mail us at email@melbay.com

1 2 3 4 5 6 7 8 9 0

For centuries the guitar has been the king of the fretted instruments. At no time in its history was it as great in prominence as it is today. At no time in the life of the guitar has there been so many styles played as proficiently as today.

We have the moden plectrum, the electric spanish, the country-western, flamenco and classic.

The classic guitar is at the height of its popularity today. The style of instrument, type of music and technique of playing has not changed radically in the past hundred years. The music of Carcassi, Aguado, Carulli, Sor and Tarrega is still tops in literature and is played beautifully by the leading artists today.

The greatest difficulty for the beginner has been the lack of an effective approach to that literature. The creation of this method of classic guitar playing has been to make the road to great literature an easy one.

It is essential that you employ the companion folio to this volume. "The Mel Bay Folio of Classic Guitar Solos" and play the designated selections as recommended throughout this first volume of the Mel Bay Classic Guitar Method.

TUNING THE GUITAR

The six open strings of the guitar will be of the same pitch as the six notes shown in the illustration of the piano keyboard. Note that five of the strings are below the middle C of the piano keyboard.

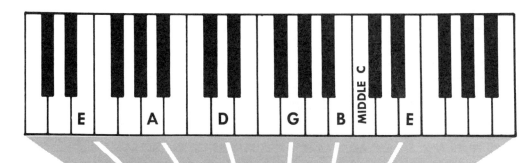

PIANO NOTATION

E A D G B E

6 5 4 3 2 1

GUITAR NOTATION

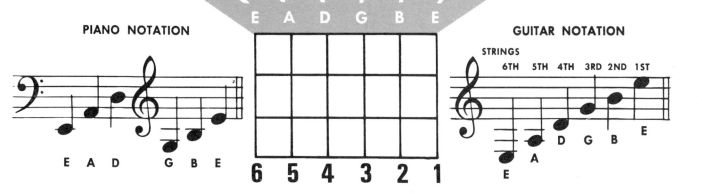

ANOTHER METHOD OF TUNING

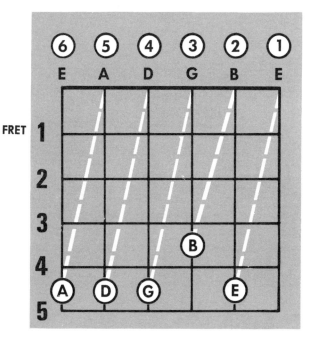

1. Tune the 6th string in unison to the **E** or twelfth white key to the LEFT of MIDDLE C on the piano.

2. Place the finger behind the fifth fret of the 6th string. This will give you the tone or pitch of the 5th string. (**A**)

3. Place finger behind the fifth fret of the 5th string to get the pitch of the 4th string. (**D**)

4. Repeat same procedure to obtain the pitch of the 3rd string. (**G**)

5. Place finger behind the FOURTH FRET of the 3rd string to get the pitch of the 2nd string. (**B**)

6. Place finger behind the fifth fret of the 2nd string to get the pitch of the 1st string. (**E**)

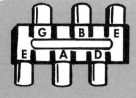

PITCH PIPES

Pitch pipes with instructions for their usage may be obtained at any music store. Each pipe will have the correct pitch of each guitar string and are recommended to be used when a piano is not available.

THE RUDIMENTS OF MUSIC

THE STAFF: Music is written on a STAFF consisting of FIVE LINES and FOUR SPACES. The lines and spaces are numbered upward as shown:

5TH LINE	
4TH LINE	4TH SPACE
3RD LINE	3RD SPACE
2ND LINE	2ND SPACE
1ST LINE	1ST SPACE

THE LINES AND SPACES ARE NAMED AFTER LETTERS OF THE ALPHABET.

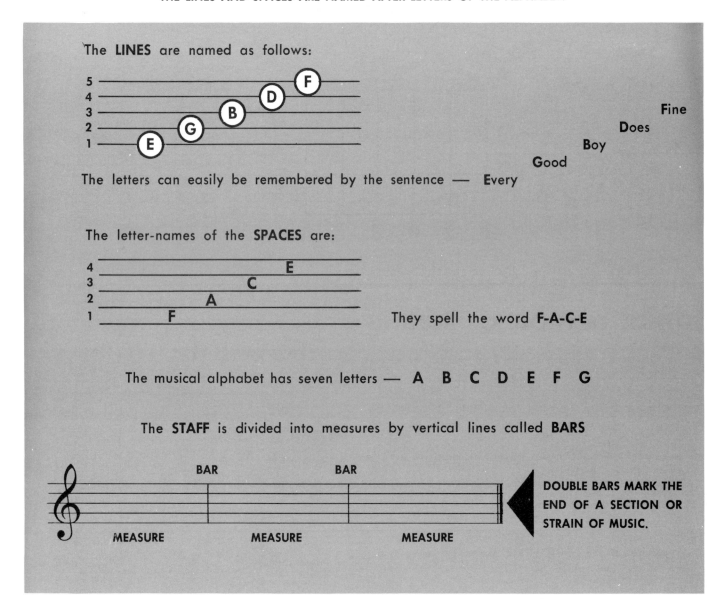

The **LINES** are named as follows:

5 4 3 2 1 — E G B D F

The letters can easily be remembered by the sentence — Every Good Boy Does Fine

The letter-names of the **SPACES** are:

4 3 2 1 — F A C E

They spell the word **F-A-C-E**

The musical alphabet has seven letters — **A B C D E F G**

The **STAFF** is divided into measures by vertical lines called **BARS**

BAR   BAR

MEASURE   MEASURE   MEASURE

DOUBLE BARS MARK THE END OF A SECTION OR STRAIN OF MUSIC.

THE CLEF:

THIS SIGN IS THE TREBLE OR G CLEF.

THE SECOND LINE OF THE TREBLE CLEF IS KNOWN AS THE G LINE. MANY PEOPLE CALL THE TREBLE CLEF THE G CLEF BECAUSE IT CIRCLES AROUND THE G LINE.

ALL GUITAR MUSIC WILL BE WRITTEN IN THIS CLEF.

NOTES:

THIS IS A NOTE:

A NOTE HAS THREE PARTS. THEY ARE

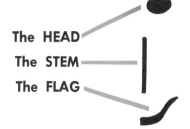

The HEAD

The STEM

The FLAG

NOTES MAY BE PLACED IN THE STAFF,   ABOVE THE STAFF,

AND BELOW THE STAFF.

A note will bear the name of the line or space it occupies on the staff.

The location of a note in, above or below the staff will indicate the Pitch.

PITCH: the highness or lowness of a tone.

TONE: a musical sound.

TYPES OF NOTES

THE TYPE OF NOTE WILL INDICATE THE LENGTH OF ITS SOUND.

THIS IS A WHOLE NOTE.
THE HEAD IS HOLLOW.
IT DOES NOT HAVE A STEM.

= 4 BEATS
A WHOLE-NOTE WILL RECEIVE FOUR BEATS OR COUNTS.

THIS IS A HALF NOTE
THE HEAD IS HOLLOW.
IT HAS A STEM.

= 2 BEATS
A HALF-NOTE WILL RECEIVE TWO BEATS OR COUNTS.

THIS IS A QUARTER NOTE
THE HEAD IS SOLID.
IT HAS A STEM.

= 1 BEAT
A QUARTER NOTE WILL RE-CEIVE ONE BEAT OR COUNT.

THIS IS AN EIGHTH NOTE
THE HEAD IS SOLID.
IT HAS A STEM AND A FLAG.

= ½ BEAT
AN EIGHTH-NOTE WILL RECEIVE ONE-HALF BEAT OR COUNT. (2 FOR 1 BEAT)

RESTS:

A REST is a sign used to designate a period of silence.

This period of silence will be of the same duration of time as the note to which it corresponds.

 THIS IS AN EIGHTH REST   THIS IS A QUARTER REST

 THIS IS A HALF REST. NOTE THAT IT LAYS ON THE LINE.

 THIS IS A WHOLE REST. NOTE THAT IT HANGS DOWN FROM THE LINE.

NOTES

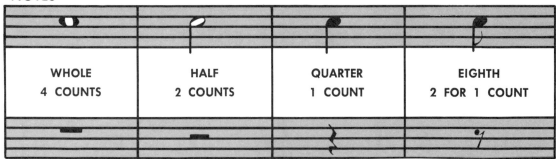

RESTS

THE TIME SIGNATURE

THE ABOVE EXAMPLES ARE THE COMMON TYPES OF TIME SIGNATURES TO BE USED IN THIS BOOK.

 THE TOP NUMBER INDICATES THE NUMBER OF BEATS PER MEASURE.

THE BOTTOM NUMBER INDICATES THE TYPE OF NOTE RECEIVING ONE BEAT.

 BEATS PER MEASURE

A QUARTER-NOTE RECEIVES ONE BEAT

 SIGNIFIES SO CALLED "COMMON TIME" AND IS SIMPLY ANOTHER WAY OF DESIGNATING $\frac{4}{4}$ TIME.

LEDGER LINES:

When the pitch of a musical sound is below or above the staff, the notes are then placed on, or between, extra lines called LEDGER LINES.

THEY WILL BE LIKE THIS:

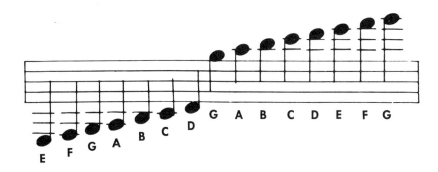

THE FINGERBOARD

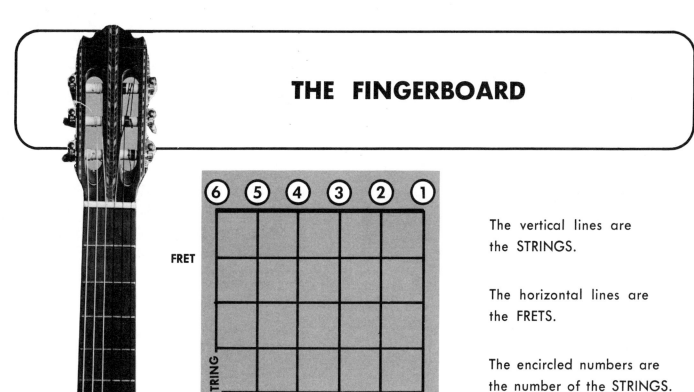

The vertical lines are the STRINGS.

The horizontal lines are the FRETS.

The encircled numbers are the number of the STRINGS.

STRING-NUMBERS: The encircled numbers **6 5 4 3 2 1** will be the numbers of the STRINGS.

CHARTS:

The charts used in this book will have the VERTICAL-LINES as the STRINGS and the HORIZONTAL-LINES as the FRETS.

Reading from left to right the strings will be:

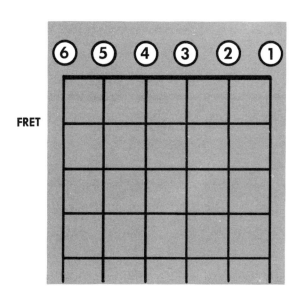

The Correct Way To Hold the Guitar

(TWO WAYS SHOWN)

1. The Left Leg Crossed over the Right.

2. Placing the Left Foot on a Small Stool.

THE RIGHT HAND
(R. H.)

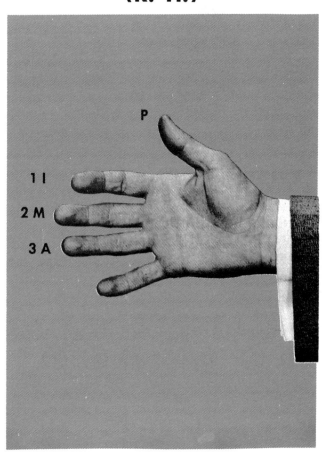

**THE RIGHT HAND FINGERS
WILL BE DESIGNATED AS**

1 = I

2 = M

3 = A

Thumb = P

**THE NAMES OF THE
R. H. FINGERS ARE:**

(English)	(ABV)	(Spanish)
1st — Index	(I)	Indice
2nd — Middle	(M)	Medio
3rd — Ring	(A)	Anular
Thumb —	(P)	Pulgar

Plucking the Strings

THE LEFT HAND
(L. H.)

The Left Hand Position

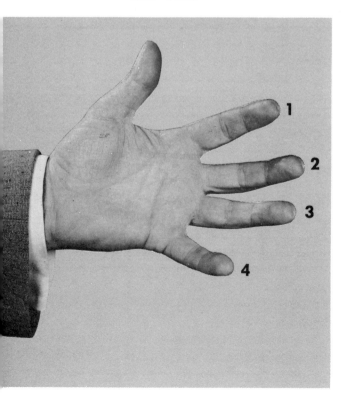

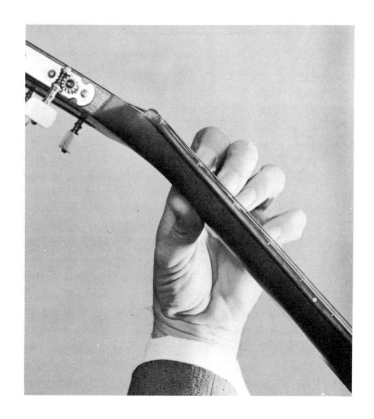

Place your fingers **firmly** on the strings **directly behind the frets.**

NOTES ON THE FIRST STRING

Note that the number of the fret and finger is identical.

NUT
FRET 1
" 2
" 3
" 4

PRESS THE FINGERS FIRMLY BEHIND THE FRETS.

NEVER PLACE THE FINGER ON THE FRETS.

E (OPEN)
F 1ST FRET 1ST FINGER
G 3RD FRET 3RD FINGER

WHOLE NOTES

A WHOLE-NOTE (○) receives FOUR BEATS.

COUNT: 1-2-3-4

HALF NOTES

A HALF-NOTE (♩) receives TWO BEATS.

COUNT: 1 2 3 4   1 2 (3 4) REST

QUARTER NOTES

A QUARTER-NOTE (♩) receives ONE BEAT.

COUNT: 1 2 3 4   1 2 3 4

NOTES ON THE SECOND STRING

THREE NOTES ON THE 2ND STRING

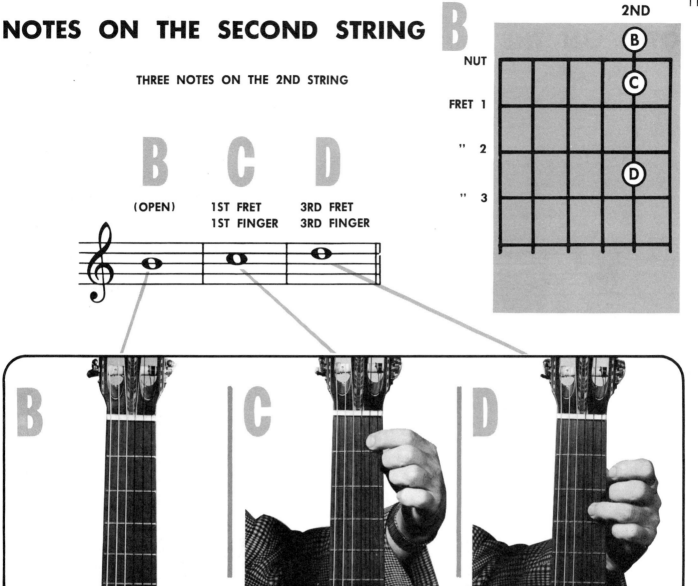

B (OPEN)   C 1ST FRET 1ST FINGER   D 3RD FRET 3RD FINGER

WHOLE NOTES

COUNT: 1 2 3 4

HALF NOTES

COUNT: 1 2 3 4

QUARTER NOTES

COUNT: 1 2 3 4

12

NOTES ON THE THIRD STRING G

TWO NOTES ON THE 3RD STRING

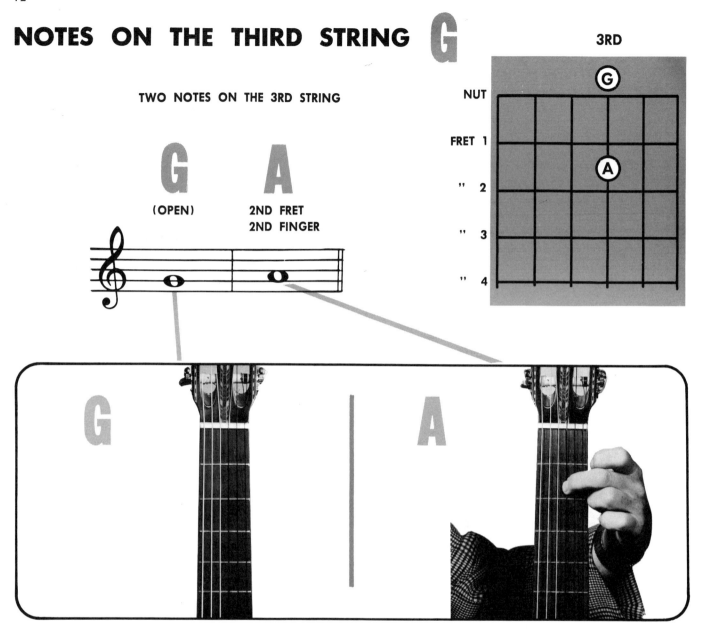

A STUDY ON THE THIRD STRING

COUNT: 1 2 3 4

Sparkling Stella

Right Hand Study

Repeat the above study until mastered.

Introducing the Right Hand Third Finger (a)

THREE-FOUR TIME

This sign ♪ **3/4** indicates THREE-FOUR time.

3 — BEATS PER MEASURE.
4 — TYPE OF NOTE RECEIVING ONE BEAT (quarter note).

In THREE-FOUR time, we will have three beats per measure.

DOTTED HALF NOTES

A dot (•) placed behind a note increases its value by one-half.

A dotted half-note (♩•) will receive three beats.

♩ = 2 COUNTS   ♩• = 3 COUNTS

The Merry Men

NOTES ON THE FOURTH STRING

THREE NOTES ON THE 4TH STRING

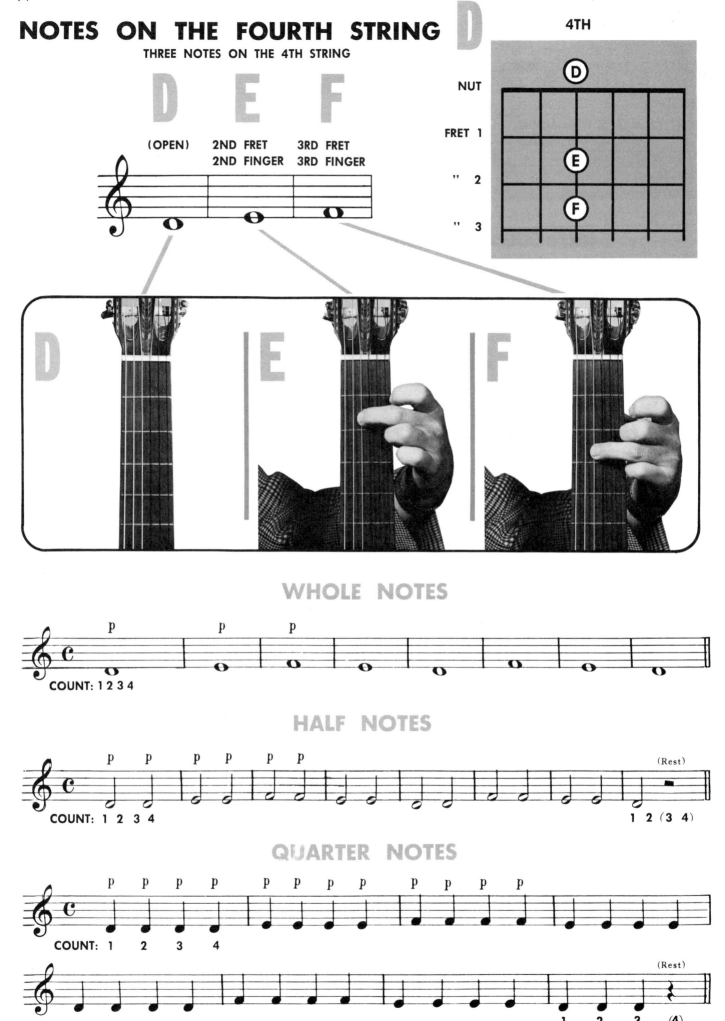

WHOLE NOTES

COUNT: 1 2 3 4

HALF NOTES

COUNT: 1 2 3 4   1 2 (3 4)

QUARTER NOTES

COUNT: 1   2   3   4   1   2   3   (4)

NOTES ON THE FIFTH STRING A

THREE NOTES ON THE 5TH STRING

NOTES ON THE SIXTH STRING

THREE NOTES ON THE 6TH STRING

WHOLE NOTES

HALF NOTES

QUARTER NOTES

Two Solos

The following solos will be played on the 6th, 5th, and 4th strings.

Play slowly at first keeping the time as evenly as possible.

Do not raise the left hand fingers from the strings until absolutely necessary.

How Can I Leave Thee

Andantino

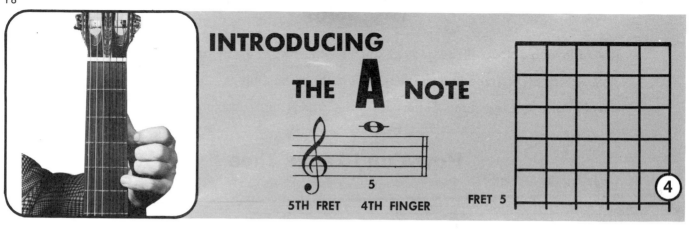

INTRODUCING THE A NOTE

5TH FRET   4TH FINGER   FRET 5

The First String Waltz

THE NOTES ON THE GUITAR IN THE FIRST POSITION

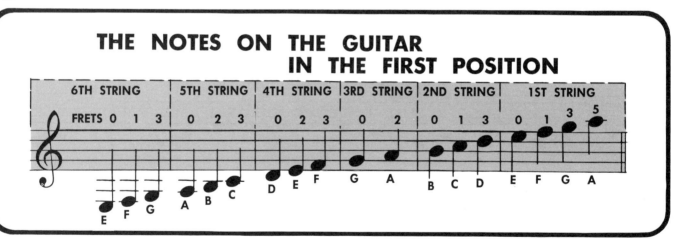

6TH STRING	5TH STRING	4TH STRING	3RD STRING	2ND STRING	1ST STRING
FRETS 0 1 3	0 2 3	0 2 3	0 2	0 1 3	0 1 3 5
E F G	A B C	D E F	G A	B C D	E F G A

Sixpence

PICK-UP NOTES

One or more notes at the beginning of a strain before the first measure are referred to as pick-up notes.

The rhythm for pick-up notes is taken from the last measure of the selection and the beats are counted as such. Note the three beats in the last measure of the following study.

A Study Introducing the Pick-up Note

COUNT: 4   1   2   3   4

Etude

A Study By Aguado

WHEN TWO OR MORE NOTES ARE WRITTEN ON THE SAME STEM, PLAY THEM AS ONE.

Example

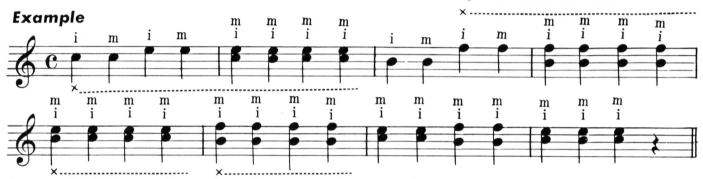

(x--------): Hold L. H. finger down. Never raise fingers until necessary.

In the above Example, play the double notes with the first finger of the R. H., plucking the lower note, and the second finger of the R. H. plucking the top note.

In the following Studies, play the lower notes with the R. H. Thumb (P).

Watch the L. H. fingering.

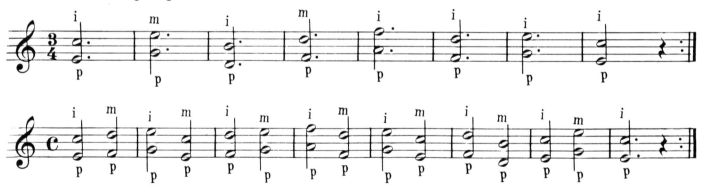

Play the Lower Notes with the Thumb (P)

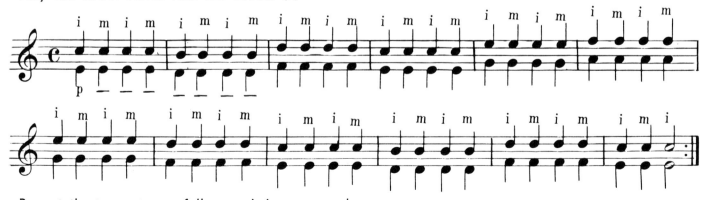

Repeat the top notes as follows: mimi, mama and amam.

Follow the Leader

Mel Bay

COUNT: 2 3 4

In the following Studies, play the lower notes with the Right Hand Thumb.

Watch the Left Hand fingering.

Alpine Echoes

Mel Bay

Waltz

Mel Bay

In the following studies the lower notes are played with the thumb.

Hold each note for its full time value.

A Study

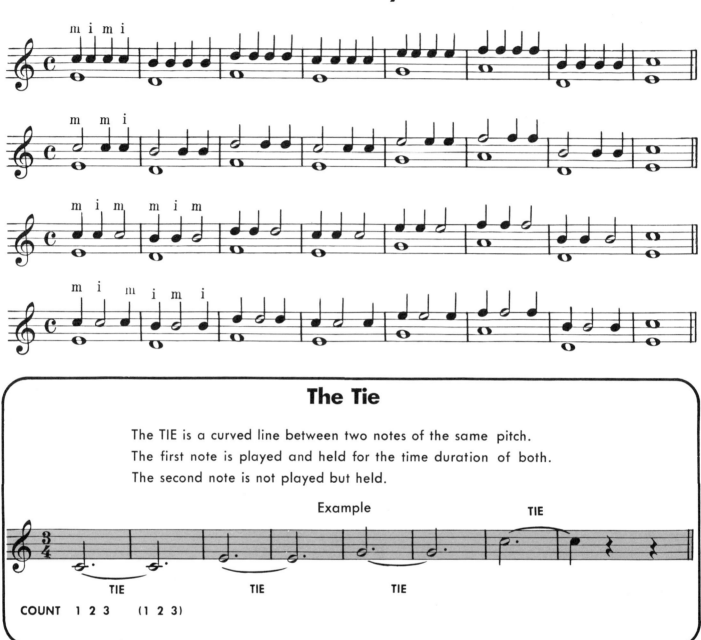

The Tie

The TIE is a curved line between two notes of the same pitch.
The first note is played and held for the time duration of both.
The second note is not played but held.

The Tie Waltz

CHORDS

A MELODY is a succession of single tones.

A CHORD is a combination of tones sounded together.

TONES IN A MELODY.

THE SAME TONES AS A CHORD.

We will construct our chords by playing the chordal tones separately as in a melody and **without raising the fingers**, striking them together.

The Chord Waltz

MEL BAY

The Builder

MEL BAY

Small Chord Etude

MEL BAY

/ / / = REPEAT CHORD

Practice the above etude until it can be played without missing a beat.

*Note that the first finger holds down two notes (C-F) in the second chord.

Bass Solos With Chord Accompaniment

When playing bass solos with chord accompaniment you will find the solo with the stems turned **downward** and the accompaniment with the stems turned **upward**.

Unless otherwise shown, play the bass with the R. H. Thumb and the chords with the R. H. 1st, 2nd, and third fingers.

Example

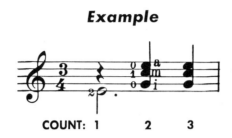

COUNT: 1   2   3

In the example shown above you see the dotted half-note (E) with the stem downward. It is played on the count of **one** and is **held** for counts **two** and **three**.

The quarter rest over the dotted half-note indicates that there is **no chord accompaniment at the count of one**. The chords with the stems upward are played on the counts of **two** and **three**.

Bass Solo With Chord Accompaniment

MEL BAY

Little Minuet

Adaptation of a
melody by CARCASSI

CHORDS IN THE KEY OF C MAJOR

The key of C has three principal chords. They are C, F, and G7.

C   F   G₇

The circles indicate the positions to place your fingers.

Numerals inside circles indicate the fingers.

(x) over the strings means that the strings are **not** to be played.

(o) over the strings indicates the strings to be played open.

Place fingers on positions indicated by the circles and strike them all together.

Musical Notation of the Chords

Accompaniment Styles

Alternate Basses

In Three-Four Time

THE KEY OF C
All music studied so far in this book has been in the Key of C.

That means that the notes have been taken from the C Scale (shown at right) and made into melodies.

It is called the C Scale because the first note is C and we proceed through the musical alphabet until C reappears. C-D-E-F-G-A-B-C.

We will cover the subject of keys and scales more thoroughly in the Theory and Harmony Chapters appearing later on in this course.

At present we will deal only with basic fundamentals.

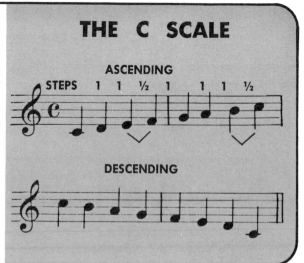

STEPS

A Half-Step is the distance from a given tone to the next higher or lower tone. On the Guitar the distance of a Half-Step is ONE FRET.

A Whole-Step consists of TWO Half-Steps.

The distance of a Whole-Step on the Guitar is TWO FRETS.

The C Scale has two half-steps. They are between E-F and B-C.

Note the distance of one fret between those notes. The distances between C-D, D-E, F-G, G-A, and A-B are Whole-Steps.

Whole-Steps and Half-Steps are also referred to as Whole-Tones and Half-Tones. We will refer to them as Whole-Steps and Half-Steps.

CHROMATICS

The alteration of the pitches of tones is brought about by the use of symbols called CHROMATICS. (Also referred to as ACCIDENTALS)

The Sharp ♯ THE SHARP PLACED BEFORE A NOTE RAISES ITS PITCH ½-STEP OR ONE FRET.

The Flat ♭ THE FLAT PLACED BEFORE A NOTE LOWERS ITS PITCH ½-STEP OR ONE FRET.

The Natural ♮ THE NATURAL RESTORES A NOTE TO ITS NORMAL POSITION. IT CANCELS ALL ACCIDENTALS PREVIOUSLY USED.

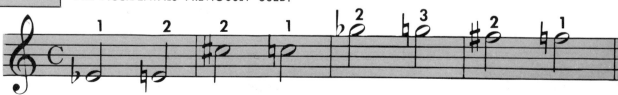

Tempo

Tempo is the **rate of speed** of a musical composition.

Three types of tempo used in this book will be:

ANDANTE: A slow easy pace.   MODERATO: Moderate.   ALLEGRO: Lively.

In the following selections pluck the notes with the downward stems with the thumb. Play the top notes as indicated.

Minuetto

GEBAUR, Opus 10
Arr. by MEL BAY

Dawn

MAZAS-BAY

THE EIGHTH NOTE

An eighth note receives one-half beat. (One quarter note equals two eighth notes).

An eighth note will have a head, stem, and flag. If two or more are in successive order they may be connected by a bar. (See Example).

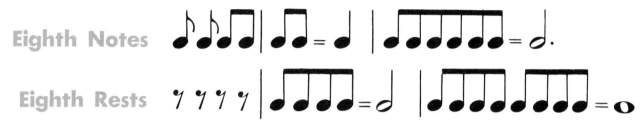

The Scale In Eighth Notes

COUNT: 1 & 2 & 3 & 4 &

A Daily Scale Study

MEL BAY

COUNT: 1 & 2 & 3 & 4 &

The above study should be played slowly with a gradual increase of speed until a moderate tempo has been reached. It is an excellent daily exercise.

A Study In Eights

THE KEY OF A MINOR
(Relative to C Major)

Each Major key will have a Relative Minor key.

The Relative Minor Scale is built upon the **sixth tone** of the Major Scale.

The Key Signature of both will be the same.

The Minor Scale will have the same number of tones (7) as the Major.

The difference between the two scales is the arrangement of the whole-steps and half-steps.

There are **three forms** of the minor scale: 1. PURE or NATURAL, 2. HARMONIC, 3. MELODIC.

The A Minor Scale
Natural (Pure)

Harmonic
The 7th tone is raised one half-step ascending and descending.

Melodic
The 6th and 7th tones are raised one half-step ascending and lowered back to their normal pitch descending.

A Visit to the Relatives

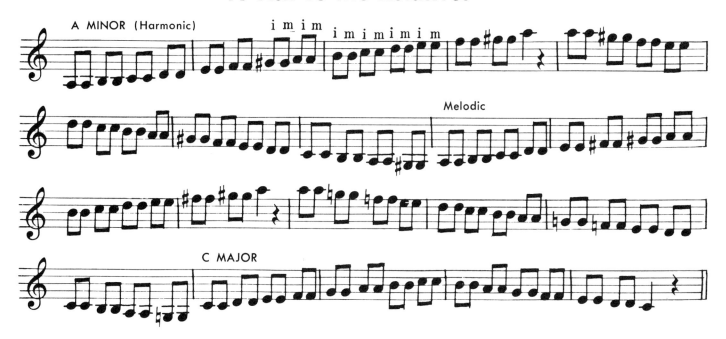

THE CHORDS IN THE KEY OF A MINOR

M = Minor

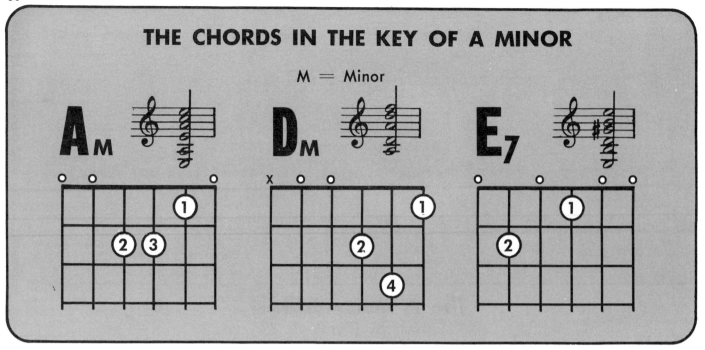

Accompaniment Styles in A Minor

This sign **%** indicates that the previous measure is to be repeated.

In the following study hold the chords as indicated, playing the melody from those chords.

Etude

Waltz

CARULLI

32

Playtime

PLEYEL
Arr. by MEL BAY

Moderato

Balkan Nights

MEL BAY

Moderato

A Daily Scale Study in A Minor

Rain Drops

First and Second Endings

Sometimes two endings are required in certain selections . . one to lead back into a repeated section and one to close it.

They will be shown like this:

The first time play the bracketed ending 1. Repeat the chorus.

The second time skip the first ending and play ending No. 2.

Cradle Song

JOHANN BRAHMS
Arr. by MEL BAY

Right Hand Study

Finger Gymnastics

The following exercises have a two-fold purpose.

(1) Training the individual fingers to perform independently of each other.

(2) Acquainting the student with the technic of position playing that will be an important part of this course.

The first finger should be held down throughout these exercises.

Repeat the above Gymnastics using the following R. H. Patterns:

①— m i m i m i m i   ②— m a m a m a m a   ③— a m a m a m a m

The Blue Tail Fly

Arr. by MEL BAY

Right Hand Studies

REPEAT EACH OF THE ABOVE STUDIES UNTIL MASTERED.

Italian Air

Andantino

CARCASSI

Classic Dance

Andantino

MEL BAY

Da Capo al Fine (D.C. al Fine): Go back to the beginning and play to FINE. (The End)

Other Tempo Terms

ALLEGRETTO . . . . Lively	ADAGIO . . . . Slower than Andante
VIVANCE . . . . Very Fast	ANDANTINO . . . . Faster than Andante
PRESTO . . . . As fast as possible	LARGO . . . . Slower than Adagio
ALLEGRO MODERATO . . . . Moderately fast	LENTO . . . . As slow as possible

Play the RIGHT HAND DEVELOPMENT ETUDE using each of the Six Patterns throughout the entire number.

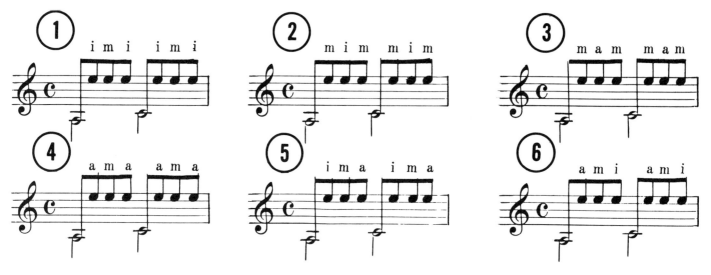

Right Hand Development Etude

See the "MEL BAY FOLIO OF CLASSIC GUITAR SOLOS"

The following Solo introduces the notes D and B being played together. This is done by playing the note D with the first finger on the third fret of the second string and playing the note B with the second finger upon the fourth fret of the THIRD STRING. For two-four time explanation see page 6.

Senorita

Senora

See the "MEL BAY FOLIO OF CLASSIC GUITAR SOLOS"

ANDANTE

F. CARULLI

The Key of G

The Key of G will have one sharp. (F♯)

It will be identified by this signature:

The F-notes will be played as shown:

2nd fret
2nd finger

4th fret
4th finger

2nd fret
2nd finger

The G Scale

Note that in order to have the half-steps falling between the seventh and eighth degrees of the scale the F must be sharped.

Our major scale pattern is then correct. (1, 1, ½, 1, 1, 1, ½.) (steps)

A Daily Drill

The Gauchos

GUITAR SOLO
Allegro

CARCASSI-BAY

CHORDS IN THE KEY OF G

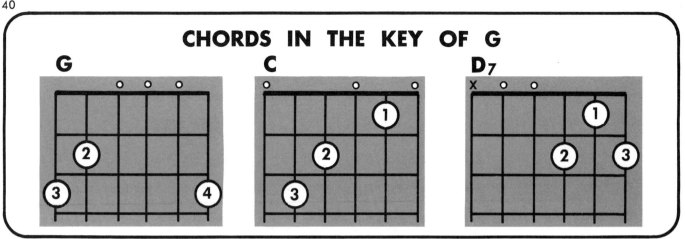

Accompaniment Styles In The Key Of G

A Scale Study

A Serenade

Moderato

MEL BAY

* Three lower notes plucked with the thumb

The following combinations should be mastered before playing the AUSTRIAN HYMN.

Austrian Hymn

HAYDN
Arr. by MEL BAY

42

The Little Prince

MAZAS
Arr. by MEL BAY

In the Evening By the Moonlight

BLAND
Arr. by MEL BAY

See the "MEL BAY FOLIO OF CLASSIC GUITAR SOLOS"

THE KEY OF E MINOR

(Relative to G Major)

The Key of E Minor will have the same key signature as G Major.

Two E Minor Scales

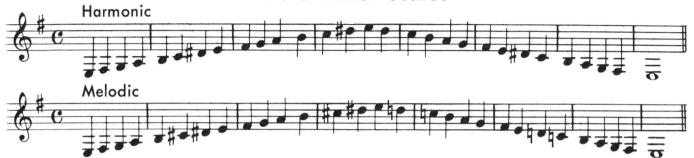

The above scales should be memorized.

THE CHORDS IN THE KEY OF E MINOR

The Chords in the Key of E Minor are:

Em   **Am**   **B7**

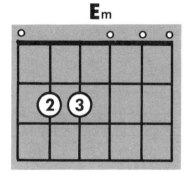 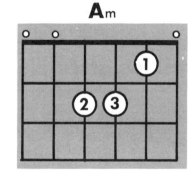 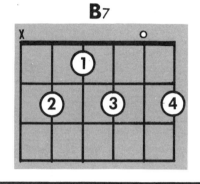

Accompaniment Styles in the Key of E Minor

Dotted Quarter Notes

A DOT AFTER A NOTE increases its Value by ONE-HALF.

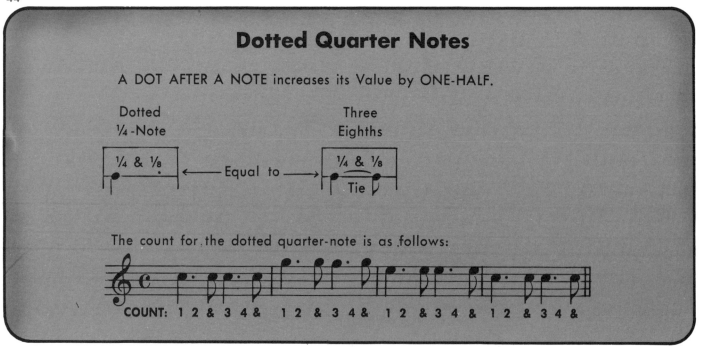

The count for the dotted quarter-note is as follows:

COUNT: 1 2 & 3 4 &   1 2 & 3 4 &   1 2 & 3 4 &   1 2 & 3 4 &

A Dotted Quarter-Note Etude

COUNT: 1 2 & 3 4 &   1 2 & 3 4 &

Right Hand Technique

Hold third finger on the D note throughout.

The Foggy, Foggy Dew

Arr. by MEL BAY

A Waltz By Sor

ANDANTE

I. K. MERTZ

A Night In Madrid

A Song By Aguado

48

Waltz in E Minor

Conchita

AGUADO

Proceed to Volume 2